THE EXTREME SURVIVAL GUIDE

THE EXTREME SURVIVAL GUIDE

Rory Storm

ELEMENT
CHILDREN'S BOOKS

SHAFTESBURY, DORSET · BOSTON, MASSACHUSETTS · MELBOURNE, VICTORIA

To my mum and dad.

© Element Children's Books 1999
Text © Rory Storm 1999
Illustrations © Mei Lim 1999

First published in Great Britain in 1999 by
Element Children's Books
Shaftesbury, Dorset SP7 8BP

Published in the USA in 1999 by
Element Books, Inc.
160 North Washington Street,
Boston MA 02114

Published in Australia in 1999 by
Element Books and distributed by
Penguin Australia Limited,
487 Maroondah Highway, Ringwood,
Victoria 3134

Cover design by Mandy Sherliker.
Typeset by Dorchester Typesetting Group Ltd.
Printed and bound in Great Britain by J W Arrowsmith, Bristol

British Library Cataloguing in Publication data available.
Library of Congress Cataloging in Publication data available.

ISBN 1 902618 33 5

Contents

I bet if I were to ask you to come up with a survival story, you'd imagine something dramatic like an attack by a grizzly bear, or being lost for days in a blizzard on the hills.

But did any of you think about how you'd survive if you were trapped in your bedroom by a house fire? Or what you'd do if the driver of your school bus collapsed at the wheel?

Surviving comes in many guises. It's not simply about you against the elements. It's to do with how you react in an unfamiliar and potentially dangerous situation, what inner strengths you draw on in the face of adversity, the skills you have and how you use them, not to mention courage and determination.

Of course terrible disasters can happen. Once, a plane crashed in the Andes and left a Uruguayan rugby team stranded high in the mountains in freezing conditions for over two months. After their supplies of chocolate and on-board snacks had run out, they were forced to eat their dead comrades to survive. Once they realized that all rescue attempts had been called off, they tried to get off the mountain themselves. Can you believe it took five attempts for two survivors to reach help and to get the other fourteen remaining passengers rescued? Would you have had the determination to try to find a way five times? That takes courage, doesn't it?

Special Services

Elite troops from the special services are put through rigorous training to prepare for just such eventualities as exposure to the extremes of climate and terrain. During Arctic training, the British SAS and paratroopers have to sleep in holes dug in the snow with no other protection from the sub-zero temperatures than their clothing. They're also expected to jump into the icy waters carrying their bergens[1] and to clamber out by themselves using an ice pick. Doesn't sound like much fun does it?

Meanwhile, the US Marines learn the skills of jungle survival in the highly treacherous rain forests of South America. Here they're taught which plants will keep them alive and which will poison them, which bugs to eat and which ones to avoid, and how to set traps and travel undetected. Then they are left alone to fend for themselves for days.

[1]A bergen is a British military rucksack.

Essential Survival Skills

Ideally, you'll never have to live off bugs and worms for a week. But just in case you ever find yourself in a dangerous situation, this book is going to give you basic survival skills such as how to build a shelter and how to make a fire. We'll also look at ways in which you can help others who are in danger and possibly save lives with some basic first aid. As if all that weren't enough, we've added some real-life spine-tingling survival stories. And, just to keep you on your toes, there will be quizzes and questionnaires to test your survival knowledge as well.

Is Luck on Your Side?

Finally, let's not forget that luck plays its part in survival as well. Like the time in October 1998 when a 23-year old French shepherd called Christian Raymond was tending his flock more than 6,000 feet (2,000 meters) up a mountain. While trying to rescue two trapped sheep, he slipped down a steep, grassy bank. He realized he was in big trouble so he dialed the emergency Alpine rescue services using his mobile phone. He had just got through to the operator when the connection failed and Mr. Raymond lost his grip, slipping over the edge of the ravine. He just managed to hold on to some rock and grass at the edge of the cliff. Luckily, his phone slithered down the slope too and ended up near his face. He realized that he could dial the emergency number by pressing the redial button with his nose.

The operator didn't believe him at first but when he started screaming, a helicopter was sent out. Mr. Raymond was rescued 17 minutes later. "I could have held on for another two or three minutes, but no longer. The muscles in my arms were seizing up," he said. "I realize I've been lucky. You know, in some parts of the mountain, the portables don't work!"

And who knows, one day it could be you facing a life-threatening situation. Would you be calm enough and sharp enough to get out of trouble? Let's find out, shall we?

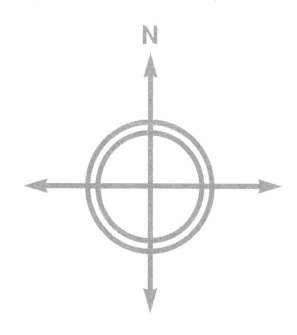

◇ CHAPTER TWO ◇

Before you flick to the juicy real-life survival stories, let's see just how smart and ready for action you are yourself. You can find out how you scored at the end. (No cheating now!)

Don't worry if you get a low score. By the end of this book, I'm sure you'll be getting straight As, and you should be ready to tackle just about any survival situation.

1. **Your car gets a flat tire, veers off the road and crashes in the middle of the desert. You're the only survivor. Should you:**

   a. Wait by the vehicle wreckage for help?
   b. Set off walking to get help?
   c. Try to repair the car?

2. Most accidents in the mountains happen

a. Between 7 a.m. and 9 a.m.

b. Between 2 p.m. and 4 p.m.

c. Between 10 p.m. and midnight.

3. You find yourself in open country in a heavy thunderstorm. Where is the best place to seek shelter?

a. In the lee of a rock.

b. Under a tree.

c. In a storm drain.

4. What is the best method of lighting a fire in the wilds?

a. Gasoline.

b. Flame-thrower.

c. Tinder and match.

5. Salt is essential for human survival. You lose salt through sweat and urine. If no direct salt supply is available, the best way to get it is:

a. From drinking seawater.

b. From animal blood.

c. From potato chips.

6. Does a compass point to

a. True north?

b. Magnetic north?

7. If the scale of your map is 1:50,000, each measure on the map represents a distance

   a. 50 times greater on the ground.

   b. 5,000 times greater on the ground.

   c. 50,000 times greater on the ground.

---

8. Which clouds bring heavy rain?

   a. Altocumulus clouds.

   b. Cumulonimbus clouds.

   c. Stratus clouds.

---

9. A red sky in the morning indicates:

   a. A storm is approaching.

   b. Rain is unlikely.

   c. There's a rainbow.

---

10. At night, how long does it take the eyes to get accustomed to darkness?

   a. One minute.

   b. 10-20 minutes.

   c. 30-40 minutes.

---

11. In Morse code, ··· − − − ··· (three dots, three dashes, three dots) means

   a. Help!

   b. Save our souls.

   c. Stop or (I'll) shoot.

12. The Heimlich maneuver is

a. A military operation in the Second World War.

b. A nautical knot.

c. A first-aid technique.

Did You Survive?

Shall we see how you got on with our dirty dozen? Award yourself a point for every correct answer.

Answers

1a. It is much easier for a rescue party to find a large wreckage area than to find a small individual in the vastness of the desert. You can also use the vehicle for shelter in the cold desert nights. Unless you're a qualified mechanic, I don't reckon your chances are very high of getting a crashed vehicle back on the road again, do you?

2b. Many people have accidents on the way back from an adventure in the mountains. By the end of a day's walking, they are tired and not as careful as they are earlier in the day while still fresh. Unless they have been lost on the mountain or delayed for some reason, very few walkers are mad enough to still be out in the mountains at night, so statistically, there are most accidents between 2 p.m. and 4 p.m.

3a. Head for the rock every time. If you shelter under a tree you're asking to get struck by lightning. If you chose 3c, just think about it for a minute. What's a storm drain for? Yes, to divert excessive rainfall. So what's likely to come rushing down your cozy hideaway? You got it: a devastating torrent of water. NEVER go near storm drains.

4c. Tinder and match is far and away the best and safest way to light a fire in the open. Gasoline is highly flammable and extremely dangerous and I strongly recommend that you never touch it — leave it to adults and they should exercise extreme care too. If you have absolutely no alternative, carefully soak a rag and light this. Never ever pour gasoline directly on a fire unless you want to go up in flames. And a flame-thrower is not something you should even think about taking into the wilderness.

5b. Well, when needs must . . . you might as well get your salt supply second-hand, as it were, from animal blood, which is an excellent source of minerals. Drinking seawater will make you crazy (no, I mean it). Potato chips would be nice, but how often do you find them in the wilds?

6b. A compass points to magnetic north. The difference between magnetic and true north varies according to where you are in the world.

7c. 1:50,000 means that each measure on the map represents a distance 50,000 times greater on the ground. Seems obvious now, doesn't it?

8b. Cumulonimbus clouds are low, menacing thunder clouds which bring hail, strong winds, thunder, and lightning. Altocumulus clouds are fair-weather clouds which often appear after a storm. Stratus clouds are not normally rain clouds but can produce a fine drizzle.

9b. Remember the old saying, "Red sky at night, shepherd's delight. Red sky in the morning, shepherd's warning." Well, it's quite true. A red sky in the morning usually indicates that a storm or shower is on its way whereas red sky at night means there is little moisture in the atmosphere so rain is unlikely within the next couple of hours. You get a rainbow when the sun is shining while it's raining.

10c. Surprisingly, it takes more than half an hour for the eyes to grow accustomed to darkness. Once you've achieved this, try to protect the eyes from the light. If you need to use a flash-light, keep one eye closed so that the night vision in that eye is not impaired.

11a. SOS is the universal code for Help! The letters don't stand for anything. They were chosen because they're easy to remember and transmit in Morse.

12c. This is a highly successful technique to help someone who is choking. Ask someone to show you.

Scoring

So, was it harder than you thought or did you find it a cinch? Whatever your score, there's always plenty more to learn in the field of survival. I've been out there practicing survival skills most of my life and I'm still discovering new tips and techniques.

0-4 points:

The only way to look at it is that you've got plenty of room for improvement. I sure hope you're scoring better by the end of this book, though, or I won't be coming on any adventures with you!

4-8 points:

Well, that's more like it. You've obviously got a grasp of the basics but could do with honing your skills and picking up a few more.

8-12 points:

Well done! You've certainly been paying attention at Scout camp. But don't rest on your laurels (unless there's nothing else to sleep on!) because there are plenty more survival tips to pick up.

Whatever your score, I think it's time to roll up our sleeves and get down to the serious business of surviving, don't you?

CHAPTER THREE

BASIC SURVIVAL SKILLS – OUTDOORS

Whether it's owing to an accident, exhaustion, or bad weather, you could find yourself stranded when out adventuring. It's happened to the best of us. If it looks as if you're going to have to spend at least a night exposed to the elements, then turn your thoughts to making a basic shelter while there's still enough daylight to see by.

Making a Shelter

In the absence of a tent, check to make sure there's no natural shelter available. You'd feel pretty foolish if you spent hours making a shelter only to find that you're right next to a snug, warm cave.

Picking the Right Spot

Build your shelter in the right place and it'll do you

proud. I've spent many a long night safe and dry in a hastily erected basher[1] sheltering from the worst conditions. And, to tell you the truth, I prefer sleeping outside to a stuffy hotel room any day!

Bear in mind:

◆ Find somewhere that's sheltered from the wind, near water and with plenty of wood nearby, if possible.

◆ Avoid deep hollows or valley bottoms, where the ground tends to be wet and marshy.

◆ Avoid solitary trees, which attract lightning.

◆ Don't get too close to water or you'll be

troubled by insects and could be wiped out by flash floods in heavy rainfall.

◆ Choose flat ground, if possible.

A Roof Over Your Head

Using a sheet of plastic or canvas, a waterproof poncho, or a groundsheet, plus some cord, rope, or twine, you can make a good looking basher.

EXTREME

SURVIVAL TIP

A wrecked plane or vehicle can make a good shelter, but avoid it if there's a risk of fire or fuel tanks exploding. Wait until it's burned out before attempting any salvage.

[1]A shelter made from waterproof sheeting.

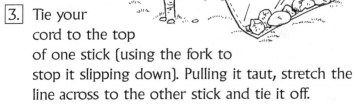

1. Find two sticks that are roughly the same length, preferably with a fork at the end.

2. Push them into the ground.

3. Tie your cord to the top of one stick (using the fork to stop it slipping down). Pulling it taut, stretch the line across to the other stick and tie it off.

4. Throw the sheeting over the line and weight down the edges with heavy rocks.

If you don't have any materials at all, don't panic. You can make use of natural cover such as trees, hollows, and rocks to provide a bit of shelter. In completely open country, sit with your back to the wind and place any equipment you have, or anything you can lay your hands on, behind you as a windbreak.

EXTREME SURVIVAL TIP

Never lie directly on the cold ground if you can help it. If you don't have a waterproof groundsheet or bivvy bag,[2] use dry grass, or even old newspaper as bedding.

[2] A waterproof sleeping bag.

Making A Fire

If you can light a fire anywhere under any conditions, then you'll always have a source of warmth and protection and a means of cooking and signaling.

Extreme Facts

There's a spider in Australia that likes nothing better than to hide inside empty boots. When the unfortunate camper puts them on next morning, he or she gets a nasty, poisonous bite which, in extreme cases, can kill. Many harmless creepy-crawlies also like to shelter from the cold in a nice warm boot. So when you climb into bed at night, keep your boots dry and beastie-free by hanging them upside down on two sticks stuck in the ground under your shelter.

A wigwam fire

1. Clear an area of leaves, twigs, dry grass, etc., until you've got a bare earth surface.

2. Make a small pile of kindling (twigs, small sticks, and small, dry leaves).

3. Around this, build a wigwam shape with thin but longer sticks.

4. Put a ball of tinder (dry grass, dead leaves, bark) inside the kindling. Light the tinder with a match. The kindling will soon catch.

5. Once your fire is lit, it will burn fiercely. The wigwam will collapse into a pile of hot, burning embers. Now, very carefully, add more sticks.

Putting Out a Fire Safely

Unless watched at all times, fires can spread easily and become dangerous.

◆ Once the fire has died down, pour water over it. (Dirty dishwater works well if you're at camp.)

◆ You can use sand or earth to sprinkle over the fire to stop it smoking and put it out.

◆ When the fire is cold, scrape the embers with a stick until they have all crumbled into ash. But be careful, they can be extremely hot.

EXTREME

SURVIVAL TIP

When it's windy, dig a trench and light your fire in it. Or encircle your fire with rocks to save fuel.

If the ground is wet or snowy, lay a platform of green logs covered with earth or stones and then build your fire on that.

Lighting a Fire

Matches are far and away the easiest way to start a fire, but if you don't have any, try the following:

1. Flint:
   Strike the flint with anything made of steel and sparks should fly.

2. Sunlight through a lens:

◆ Use a magnifying glass, spectacles, or a camera lens.

◆ Focus the sun's rays to form a tiny bright spot of light. Keep it steady and shield it from the wind.

◆ Blow gently until it glows.

3. Hand drill:

◆ Cut a V-shaped notch in any hard wood, preferably a flat piece so you can lay it down like a baseboard and keep both hands free.

◆ Put a little tinder in the V notch.

◆ Make a slight depression or small hole at the tip of the V.

◆ Use a stick made of softwood (with a soft core) for a spindle, and place it in the hole you made.

◆ Roll the spindle between the palms of your hands, running hands down it as you go to press it into the depression.

◆ When the friction makes the spindle tip glow red, blow gently to light the tinder.

Cooking on a Fire

Use the fire to boil water, then let the flames die down and use the embers and hot ash for cooking. Never leave your fire unattended during cooking. After all, you've got enough to contend with just surviving, without having to fight fires too!

Implements

Some foods such as fish can be cooked directly in the embers of a fire, usually wrapped in something suitable to stop them burning (in the absence of aluminum foil, use large green leaves or even moss). Otherwise you can use a sharpened stick for a skewer (ideal for vegetable kebabs) or like a toasting fork (good for sausages, bread, and marshmallows).

If you have a billy can, here's how to make a pot rest so you can cook a proper meal.

Extreme Facts

All freshwater fish can be eaten. Those under 5 cm (2 inches) long need no preparation — cook and eat whole. Larger fish need gutting.

Special Services-style pot rod

1. Drive a sturdy, forked stick into the ground near the fire.

2. Rest a longer stick across the fork with the top end over the fire.

3. Drive the bottom of the long stick into the ground and weight it with rocks.

4. Before putting it over the fire, cut a groove near the top to stop the pot handle from slipping off or tie on a forked stick to use as a hook.

Bugs on the menu

Insects and worms are best boiled. Mince small ones by crushing in a can. Or dry them on hot rocks, then grind into a powder to put in soups and stews. Always starve worms for a day (by keeping in an empty pot) to clear the muck out of them. Then boil them or dry them and grind into powder to thicken other food.

Try not to be squeamish – they're really not that bad. In survival training, elite troops often have to eat them raw. Cooking is a luxury!

And in Australia, a great delicacy of the Aboriginal people is the witchetty grub. It's a big, fat, white maggotlike caterpillar which they dig out from the roots of trees and eat alive. Could you bring yourself to do that? You have to be pretty darn hungry, I can tell you that!

Finding Water

Even if your food runs out, you can keep going for a very long time on water alone. So it's important that you find a source of water.

◆ Look in valley bottoms for streams. Dig in dry streambeds, the water may be just below the surface.

◆ At the coast, look for plants growing in faults on cliffs — you may find a spring.

◆ Plants often trap water in cavities. Don't forget to strain it to remove insects before drinking, though. You don't want dead flies slipping down, do you?

◆ Tie clean cloths around your legs and ankles and walk through wet vegetation (particularly in the morning when plants are covered in dew). These can then be sucked or wrung out.

◆ Melt snow a little at a time in a pot and gradually add more. If you put a lot in the pot, a hollow will form at the bottom as it melts and you'll burn your pot.

EXTREME
SURVIVAL TIP

Avoid any pool that has no vegetation growing around it or where there are dead animal bones. It may be polluted. Always boil water collected from pools.

Extreme Facts

An adult can survive only three days without water.

Collecting Rainwater

If you still can't find any water, you can always collect it when it rains. Rainwater is the cleanest natural water. Collect it when it falls by leaving out containers, or make a water collector:

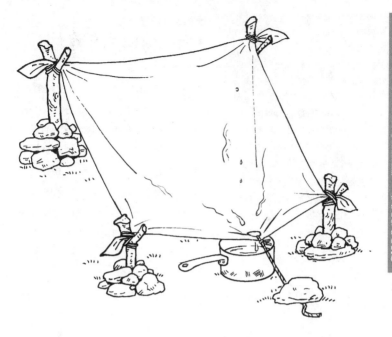

1. Lay a groundsheet or plastic sheet on the ground.

2. Use two long sticks at the back and two shorter sticks at the front (supported by rocks or guyed) to lift the sheeting off the ground, so that it forms a slope.

3. In the middle of the lower edge of the sheeting, make a hole. Tie a piece of string to this hole and weight the other end with a heavy stone. This pulls it down to make a sort of spout down which the collected rainwater will run.

4. Put a container under this spout and, hey presto, you have cold running water.

EXTREME SURVIVAL TIP

One way of making sure the water you collect is safe to drink is to boil it. If you don't have a fire, try filtering it through a sock into a bowl several times. If your socks are anything like mine, it sounds gross, I know, but it really does work.

Help Your Rescuers Find You

Almost any signal repeated three times can be used as a distress signal: three fires near to each other, or three columns of smoke; three whistles or flashes of light. Choose high points for your signals and don't build a fire among trees — it could get out of hand and it won't be seen from the air because of the trees' canopy.

If a rescue plane flies over and then turns away, don't give up hope. A search starts from the last

Extreme Facts

Stranded vehicles or crashed aircraft can provide all manner of things to help you signal for help. Tires can be burned to make a dense plume of black smoke (don't breathe it in); glass and chrome can make good reflectors; brightly colored objects like life jackets can be laid out on the ground to catch the eye.

known location and sweeps along the proposed route. The plane could be following a search pattern and may turn back again. Stay alert.

Finding Help Yourself

If you decide to try to walk out for help rather than wait to be rescued, you'll need to know what direction you're going in. Even without a map or compass, you can still find your way by using the sun. Remember the old saying, the sun rises in the east and sets in the west — well, that little nugget of info could just save your bacon.

Finding Your Way Using a Stick

1. Push a stick firmly into some flat ground.

2. In the early morning, mark the end of the shadow it makes with a stone (it will be pointing west because the sun has risen in the east).

3. Throughout the day, mark the position of the shadow. By the afternoon, the sun will move towards the west and its shadow will point east.

4. Late in the afternoon, draw a straight line between the stones. This line will point east-west.

5. Now draw a line at right angles to this line, straight through the base of the stick. This new line runs north-south.

Using the first east-west line you made, if you stand facing east, north will be on your left and south will be on your right.

Finding Your Way Using Your Watch

1. Hold watch horizontal.
2. Point the hour hand at the sun.
3. South lies halfway between the hour hand and the 12 o'clock position.

In the southern hemisphere, use the same method, but it is north that lies halfway between the two positions.

Finding Your Way Unaided

Unfortunately, on a cloudy day, you're somewhat stuck without a compass! However, there are a few tips to follow:

◆ If you are completely lost, find a waterway and follow it downstream (the direction the water is moving in) until you find a populated area.

◆ Try to skirt around dense vegetation such as woods and forests — it's too easy to get disoriented when you can't see very far.

◆ Once on high ground, stick to it until you are sure you've found the best way down in the direction you want to go.

◆ Find a distant landmark and head towards it to maintain direction.

CHAPTER FOUR

BASIC SURVIVAL — HOME ALONE

I f you think it's tough out there in the great outdoors, you may be surprised to learn that there are just as many dangers lurking in our everyday environment — at home, at school, in our parks, in our pools, and on the roads! True survivalists stay alert wherever they are, not just in the wilds. When an accident or emergency happens in your normal day-to-day life, the same survivors' instincts that you used in the country must kick in. It's the same principles:

◆ Stay calm and lucid.
◆ Be decisive and act quickly.
◆ Once the immediate danger is over, get help from the professionals.

Finally, trust your heart and mind to do the right thing. Often, in a crisis, the least likely hero may draw on inner strength to act courageously.

I've met a lot of unlikely heroes and it could just as easily be you as anyone else.

The two biggest threats to local safety come from fire and water, or more precisely drowning. In the United States, 1,050 young people aged under 15 died by accidental drowning in 1997 and a further 700 died in fires. These were the top two child killers (after road accidents) for that year. The figures are just as grim in Britain. The latest statistics show that 72 percent of all fatal child accidents in the home (up to 14 years old) were from fires, with drowning claiming another 20 percent.

So let's look now at a few ways to be a survivor if you come across danger involving either of the two elements fire and water.

Fighting Fires

If you saw the film *Backdraft* — or even *Bambi* come to that — you'll know just how devastating and dangerous a fire can be. Firefighters agree that prevention is the best way to tackle fire, but failing that, a rapid response once the fire is discovered can save lives. Shall we see what we can do to help?

If You Discover a Fire in Your Home or at School

Smoke and fumes can kill — particularly the highly poisonous smoke from some furnishings. You'll only have a short period of time to get out. Use it wisely and try not to panic.

1. Raise the alarm. If possible, tell an adult.

2. Get out. If you can, close the door of the room where the fire is and close all doors behind you as you leave. Before opening a closed door, use the back of your hand to touch it. Do NOT open it if it feels warm — the fire will be on the other side.

3. Get others out too, if you can, as quickly as possible. Stay calm and your example will keep them calm too. Don't try to take anything with you — forget your personal belongings, it's really not worth the risk.

4. Get the fire service out. Go to the nearest telephone (whether a payphone or a neighbor's). Clearly state the address of the fire.

5. Stay out. Don't go back in for anything. Your life is much more precious than your toys, possessions, or even your pets. (I know it's hard, but being brave sometimes means making tough decisions.)

EXTREME SURVIVAL TIP

Call the emergency services.

The telephone number for the fire department varies from country to country. In the United States, call 911. In Britain, ring 999 or 112.

Remember: Get out, get the fire service out, and stay out!

Extreme Facts

Smoke spreads in seconds, fire in minutes.

If You're Cut Off by Fire

I can't think of anything more frightening than being trapped in a blazing building, can you? It doesn't bear thinking about. But there are certain measures you can take, if you ever find yourself in this terrifying situation, to improve your chances of survival (and everyone else's).

Extreme Facts

In the UK, 75 children die and over 2,000 are injured each year in house fires.

1. Try to remain calm.
2. If you can't use the door because of flames or smoke, close the door and use towels, sheets or clothing to block any gaps. This will help stop smoke spreading into the room.
3. Try to make your way to the window. If the room becomes smoky, crawl commando-style along the floor where it's easier to breathe because smoke rises.

4. Open the window and try to attract the attention of others who can alert the fire service. Wait for the fire engine to arrive.

5. The fire brigade should arrive in a matter of minutes. If you are in immediate danger and your room is not too high from the ground, drop cushions or bedding to the ground below

to break your fall from the window. If you can, get out feet first and lower yourself to the full length of your arms before dropping.

EXTREME SURVIVAL TIP

Planning your escape route

If there's a fire in your home, you may have to get out in dark and difficult conditions. Escaping from a fire will be a lot easier if you have already planned your escape route and know where to go.

• Why not talk about your escape route with your mother, father, or another adult where you live? And draw an escape plan.

• Once you've worked out your route, make sure you always keep it clear of toys and other things that could block your way out.

• At bedtime, ask yourself, "Is my escape route clear?" and "Have I switched everything off? My TV, my computer?"

Extreme Facts

Survival training
Trainee firefighters are put in a blazing house in the pitch dark and expected to find their way out by crawling under the smoke. Obviously this exercise is highly supervised, but it gives them a taste of the dangerous work that's to come.

Oil-Pan Fires

If you've nagged and nagged your mother for fries or donuts, and she's finally obliged, you'd better know what to do if the pan goes up in flames. No, not to save your donuts, to save yourself and your mother!

1. Turn off the heat (only if it's safe).
2. Run a cloth under cold water and wring it out.
3. Cover the pan and leave it to cool completely for at least 30 minutes.
4. If there's any doubt about whether you can put out the fire yourself, then don't try. Leave the room, close the door and call the fire department.
5. Never put water on any kind of grease fire.

If your clothes catch fire

1. **Stop.** Don't run, as this will make the fire worse.
2. **Drop.** Get down on the floor
3. **Roll over.** This puts the flames out. Keep on rolling until you're sure.
4. **If someone else is on fire,** lay them down and roll them over to put out the flames.

Don't Let a Fire Start

Of course, it's far better to stop fires starting at all. Here are a few fire-prevention tips that are worth remembering:

◆ Don't play with matches.

◆ Don't stand or play too close to fires or heaters.

◆ Don't leave toys or clothes on, or too close to, fires and heaters.

◆ Unplug anything electrical that you've been using. Not every appliance is designed to be left switched on all the time. Play it safe: unplug it.

Are You Water-Wise?

Let's face it, water holds an irresistible attraction for many people. Whether it's a paddling pool or a swimming pool, a pond, a river, or lake, there's tons of fun to be had just messing about with water. But, it has risks. One thousand and fifty young people drowned in the United States last year in boat accidents, and from swimming, playing in the

EXTREME

SURVIVAL TIP

Diving in

Never dive into unknown water – always jump feet first. There may be hidden dangers like rocks below the surface. You can easily break your neck if you hit something hard as you dive in and, be paralyzed or killed.

water, or falling in — and that doesn't take into account those drowned in floods and other natural catastrophes.

So it pays to take a few precautions before playing around water and to know what to do if you or someone else gets into difficulties.

Always follow this Water Code:

◆ Look out for dangers before you get in the water — concealed rocks, floating rubbish, stinging jellyfish, clinging seaweed. Don't just jump in.

◆ You may be able to swim well in a warm indoor pool but that doesn't mean you can swim in cold open water. Deep water is a killer — avoid it!

◆ Check new places. Ask somebody who knows the area about hidden dangers.

◆ Don't ignore safety advice. Special flags and notices are there to warn of danger.

◆ Where possible, go with an adult who can point out dangers or help if somebody gets into trouble.

Extreme Facts

Bloodsuckers

When going through jungle training, elite troops often have to wade through rivers holding their rifles above their heads. At the next stop, they check each other for leeches. To get them off, the soldiers light a cigarette and press it on the leech, which then falls off. If you simply pull them off, they leave their jaws stuck in your flesh and these can fester and turn septic.

Ticks will also leave their mouth

Water Rescue

Here's how you can help someone in difficulty in the water:

◆ **Reach.** Use a stick, a scarf, clothes tied together, or anything else that comes to hand. Crouch low or lie down to avoid being pulled in yourself. If this is not possible, then . . .

◆ **Throw.** A rope is best because you can pull the person to safety then. Otherwise throw

something that will float, such as a ball or a plastic bottle, a lifebuoy or some wood This will keep the person afloat until help comes.

◆ **Wade.** Test the depth of the water with a long stick before wading in and then use the stick to reach out. If you're with your buddies, hold on to someone else on the bank or to a tree or root on the bank. Otherwise . . .

◆ **Row.** Use a boat if there is one nearby and if you can use it safely. Don't try to pull the person on board in case they panic and capsize the boat. Tow them to shore.

Extreme Facts

A small child can drown in just 3 inches (10 cm) of water. That's less than your hand's depth. So if you're left in charge of a kid brother or sister, be particularly watchful in the bathroom and also in the garden if there are water hazards such as paddling pools and ponds.

Extreme Facts

Every year in Britain alone, over one million children under the age of fifteen have accidents in and around the home for which they are taken to hospital.

In 1997 in the United States, 6,500 kids under fifteen died from "unintentional" injuries — that's accidents to you and me.

It's a good thing you guys are doing something practical to help prevent more accidents!

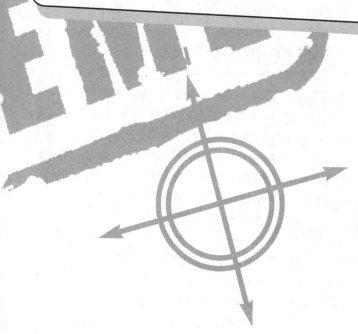

◇ CHAPTER FIVE ◇

SURVIVAL STORIES

Now that we've had a look at the principles for survival (which I hope you've tucked away in the back of your mind in case of emergencies), let's have a closer scrutiny of what happens in practice when people find themselves in real difficulties.

In the following stories and the next few chapters, you'll see just how easy it is for a day of fun and adventure to go horribly wrong. For these brave survivors, disaster and death were never far away, as you're about to find out.

An Icy Shelter

On a crisp winter day, an American father and his teenage son were skiing with a party of friends in Turkey. Engrossed in their skiing and the challenging slope they were tackling together, they became separated from the rest of the group. When they noticed,

neither of them was very concerned. They struck out to find their way back to the resort, pleased with the way they had mastered the run.

But there was an eerie silence on the mountain and they saw and heard no one. Soon they found themselves in a blizzard and it was starting to get dark. Despite his warm clothing, the son began to shiver. It grew completely dark and still there was no sign of their friends or the resort.

They moved in among the trees for shelter. The father broke off some low branches and they settled down on these as crude wooden beds for the night. They took off their boots and ate chocolate, convinced that they would be found early the next morning.

However, no help arrived, so they set off through the trees and across open snowfields, traveling all the next day. As night started to fall for the second time, they found some shelter in an icy crevasse, out of the wind.

The blizzard got worse, and they were weak with hunger. For five days and five nights, the father and son waited out the storm in their icy shelter. Dad cursed the fact that he'd recently given up smoking so he had no matches or lighter to start a fire. Snow was their only food and drink. Once or twice they heard helicopters, but they never came close enough to see them. They kept their spirits up by reminiscing over family stories and telling jokes.

Crying Wolf?

The only sound was the howling of the wind. And on one occasion they heard a scuffling noise. This was closely followed by the appearance of a hairy muzzle and burning yellow eyes at the entrance to their crevasse. It was a large wolf. It snarled at them, but they can't have looked very appetizing in their ski gear because it turned up its nose and disappeared.

On the sixth day, the weather cleared a little. The father set out to try to find help. He left his son in the safety of the crevasse with strict instructions to keep moving, in order not to freeze, and to eat the snow regularly. What must they have felt like when they said goodbye, knowing that it might be for the last time? What a tough decision to have to make — to stay together and probably perish or to split up and perhaps never see each other again. What would you have done?

Rescue

At the end of the first day, the father found a woodcutter's cottage but, to his great despair, it was empty. He collapsed with exhaustion for the night. Early the next day, he set off again, finding help farther down the mountain. A rescue squad eventually found the son, unconscious but alive.

The father and son were lost in the ice and snow for an amazing nine days in total. Of course, it's debatable whether it was the snow they ate or their love for each other that got them through their ordeal. What do you think?

SURVIVAL TIP

What if . . .

you found someone alone on a mountain who had spent several days exposed to the elements? Would you know what to do? What would your first priority be – to help the person or to go for professional help?

Well, people can die of cold. Hypothermia is caused by cold winds, damp clothing, and exhaustion. The warning signs are shivering, disorientation, lethargy, cold, pale, and dry skin, slow pulse and heartbeat . Once you've spotted these, you must act quickly. Sometimes people become irrational and violent or make illogical claims, like saying they're waiting for a UFO to come and get them.

Here's what you do if you suspect a case of hypothermia.

1. Heat the casualty up gently and slowly.

2. Wrap them in warm clothes and blankets. Keep them insulated from the ground by putting them on top of a groundsheet, coat or even a coiled rope.

3. Make sure their head is covered, preferably with a warm hat. (About half your body heat is lost through your head, so don't leave it out in the cold!)

4. If they are wearing wet clothes, forget modesty and get them into some dry clothes and/or a warm sleeping bag.

5. Even use your own body heat to warm the person up by huddling in close.

6. Give them a warm (not hot) drink and some sugary food.

7. Go for help once the person is out of danger.

Extreme Facts

Normal body temperature is 98.6°F (37°C). Your body only needs to drop to 95°F (35°C) for the first effects of hypothermia to take hold. If body temperature continues to fall below 88°F (31°C), you'll become unconscious. Death occurs at 82°F (28°C).

Runaway Bus

Danger can attend even the most commonplace journey. For one group of Welsh children, it came during their morning bus ride to school.

The school bus collected children from the villages every morning. What none of the kids realized as they rolled along the familiar route was that Reg, the driver, had suffered a fatal heart attack at the wheel. Then, one boy noticed that they were approaching a busy intersection far too fast. Suspicious, he moved to the front of the bus and saw that Reg had collapsed.

There was no time to panic. Now it was up to him to stop the runaway bus and to save his school friends.

No Brakes

First, he tried to ram on the brakes, but the driver's legs were in the way and the hand-brake was on the other side of the inert body. He tried to move the driver but, if you'll pardon the pun, Reg was a dead weight. The boy grabbed the steering wheel and, with all his strength, wrenched it to the left, narrowly avoiding the heavy traffic at the intersection and hurtling on to a minor road.

By now, although most of the kids remained oblivious, another boy had realized that the bus was on the wrong route and that something was seriously wrong. He made his way to the front of the bus and between them, the two boys used all their strength to try to steer the speeding bus down the narrow roads.

Still more danger was looming as the bus started to head back into a built-up residential area. The boys agreed to take the bus on to the grass shoulder in an effort to slow its speed. The rough bumping and jostling sent schoolchildren into a panic and many were screaming.

Head-on Collision

The soft soil slowed the bus down, but not enough, and they were running out of grass shoulder. Now they were heading straight towards the side of a house. The boys told the passengers to hold on, and braced themselves as they hit the house. Both boys were knocked unconscious by the impact.

Police and fire engines were there in minutes and the children were freed from the wreckage. No one was killed. The twist to the story is that the police initially thought that the crash was the result of an out-of-hand schoolboy prank and our champions were the suspects. Pretty soon though they discovered the real cause of the crash. Instead of joyriders, the boys were heroes. If they hadn't steered the bus away from the main road, and slowed it down enough to weaken the impact when it hit the house, there would have been many casualties. Both had nasty leg injuries from the crash but they recovered in hospital together.

Oh, and in case you're wondering, the residents of the house had already left for work so although their house was destroyed, they were not hurt.

What if . . .

you found yourself in a runaway vehicle and it was up to you to save the day? Would you know what to do? Well, according to the top rally driver Phil Price, who's had plenty of crashes and near misses in his time, there are a few golden rules to follow:

◆ First, try to stamp on the brakes or pull on the handbrake.

◆ If that fails, turn off the ignition to cut the power, and steer the vehicle until it comes to a halt.

◆ If you can see what sort of terrain lies to the side of the road and it's safe, for example a flat field, then steer off-road and use rough ground to slow the vehicle's speed. If you can't see clearly what's on the other side of the hedge then stay on the road after all There could be a steep drop or a big ditch.

◆ If a collision is unavoidable, make sure you're belted in (if possible), and brace yourself with your head protected in your arms. (Remember the position from the airline safety notices?) If you're on a bus or in a van with no seatbelts, use the seat in front to brace yourself against.

◆ Don't stand in the aisle of a bus or sit between the front seats of a car – you're likely to be thrown through the windscreen.

◆ However good it looks in the movies, never, repeat never, throw yourself from a moving vehicle. You're much safer inside.

Extreme Facts

In the United States in 1997, 31 out of every 1,000 young people aged up to fifteen years were killed in motor-vehicle accidents.

Antarctic Adventure

At the beginning of the twentieth century, Ernest Shackleton and Tom Crean made some of the most gruelling journeys in the history of exploration. One in particular stands out as an amazing feat of human endurance and survival.

Ernest Shackleton was born on February 15, 1874 in County Kildare, Ireland. He got his first taste of exploration with Captain Scott's Antarctic expedition of 1901-03 and in 1907 he led his own expedition, succeeding in traveling to within 97 miles (156 km) of the South Pole. This was closer than anybody else had yet come. Just think how frustrating it must have been to get so close but not to reach your goal. Would you have been responsible enough to turn back in order to save the lives of your crew? And would you have had the determination to try again later?

Well, Shackleton did. In 1914 he set out again in a ship called the *Endurance*. However, the expedition almost met with disaster and it was largely thanks to Shackleton's strong will and good leadership that the crew survived.

The *Endurance* was crushed in the ice of the Weddell Sea and sank, leaving the crew to survive for five long months on the ice. Although it must have looked like a suicidal mission, Shackleton finally decided to set out in a 23-foot (7-meter) lifeboat with five others to try to get help. Twenty-two men were left behind on Elephant Island and their lives depended on Shackleton and his team reaching civilization. Of course, their chances of surviving on the cold and stormy waters of the Southern Ocean, were extremely remote.

Despite all the odds, Shackleton, Crean, and their crew sailed their tiny boat for over 800 miles (about 1,300 km) across the fiercest seas in the world to make landfall on the rocky coast of South Georgia. But they were still far from safety. The only habitation, the whaling station of Stromness, was on the far side of the island, cut off by a range of mountains. Three of the crew were close to death. Summoning their last drop of strength, Shackleton, Crean, and Worsley set out and climbed for 30 miles (48 km) over the high peaks and glaciers to Stromness and safety. They did this with no equipment. This crossing has defeated many modern, well-equipped mountaineers — what does that say about Shackleton's drive and determination?

Straight after this feat of perseverance, having raised the alarm, Shackleton and Crean sailed back to Elephant Island themselves, can you believe, to rescue every last member of their team. Not a single life was lost. How cool is that?

They failed to cross the Antarctic but their story is legendary. Shackleton is regarded as perhaps the greatest of all Antarctic explorers, not just because of his achievements but because of his qualities as a leader. He inspired his men to give more than they ever dreamed possible and led by example — pushing himself beyond normal human endurance in the harshest possible conditions of the Antarctic icy wastelands. A man of remarkable spirit!

Tribute

Inspired by this great survival story, a team of leading Irish climbers and sailors followed in the footsteps of Shackleton and Crean in the Antarctic summer of 1997. They climbed some unconquered peaks on Elephant Island and then set out in a replica tiny lifeboat and sailed across the Southern Ocean to South Georgia. But of course they had better cold-weather gear and knew they could summon help if they drifted off course.

Some of the team also traversed the rugged, uninhabited interior of the island. They crossed Crean's glacier and attempted to climb Mount Roots before they reached Stromness. There they paid their respects at Shackleton's final resting place – he died here on his last expedition.

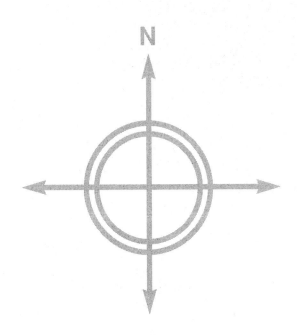

⬦ CHAPTER SIX ⬦

SURVIVAL IN TREACHEROUS WATERS

Being marooned on a desert island *à la* Robinson Crusoe always sounds so idyllic but what we all forget is that you've got to go through the horrendous experience of a shipwreck before you can become a castaway.

Adrift in Shark-infested Waters

A group of friends left Florida for the Bahamas on a two-masted, 58-foot (17.5-meter) yacht named the *Trashman*. Halfway through their voyage, the *Trashman* sank in a ferocious storm.

Debbie Scaling, an experienced sailor, and her four crewmates found themselves in a small inflatable life raft in the middle of a raging ocean. They spent the first night in the water, under the upside-down inflatable, trying to keep warm.

In the morning, they discovered that the water

was full of sharks. They wasted no time getting into the dinghy after that.

With no food, little water, and inadequate clothing, the survivors had to endure hideous sores, terrible hunger and thirst, and diving attacks from sea birds. Driven beyond endurance, two of the crew drank seawater and, little by little, went mad. With the others too weak to stop them, they swam off and didn't survive. The skipper's girlfriend, who had sustained nasty injuries during the shipwreck, also died — of exposure and gangrene.

By this time, Debbie and her sole surviving crewmate, Brad, had resigned themselves to their fate at the mercy of the sea.

The raft drifted on the open sea, circled by a school of sharks, for five days and five nights before being picked up by a Russian ship. Even as they were being rescued, a huge wave threatened to pluck the survivors from the arms of their rescuers. They were very lucky indeed to be alive and to have survived the horrors of that voyage.

How do you think you'd cope with such a living nightmare? Could you stop yourself from drinking seawater when you were so thirsty? Would you have been able to call upon those last few ounces of strength and courage to launch yourself into shark-patrolled waters to try to get to the rescue ship? It's hard to imagine, isn't it?

In truth, no one knows how they might cope under such testing conditions. However, if you are involved with boating at any level, whether it be dinghy sailing on a lake, yacht racing on the open seas, or merely rowing on the river, there are certain precautions that it's always wise to take.

Staying Afloat

◆ It's very important to make sure that your craft is in good condition and is properly equipped. Always use equipment from a reputable boat club.

◆ Never go on or near the water alone. Try to make sure there are at least three people in your group. Then, if someone gets hurt, one person can stay with him or her, while the third person goes for help.

◆ Make sure you know how to control your boat so you can maneuver out of the way of other vessels and dangers.

◆ Observe all warning signs. Otherwise you could find yourself perilously close to water hazards such as weirs, rapids, and waterfalls. And would you know what to do?

◆ Pack a first-aid kit and make sure you know how to use it.

◆ If you're on a larger boat which has a life raft, make sure it is in good condition and properly equipped with food, water, buoyancy aids, and flares.

Finally, the golden rule:

◆ Always wear a buoyancy aid or life jacket on and near the water.

Extreme Facts

Monsters of the deep

There are 300 species of shark but only 27 of these pose a threat to humans. But those 27 are very dangerous indeed (have you seen the number of teeth these monsters have?) and a few are deadly.

The largest predatory shark is the Great White, reaching a length of more than 21 feet (6 meters) and weighing up to 7,000 lb (3,200 kg).

About 50 shark attacks are reported each year, but hundreds more probably take place in remote parts of the world and are never reported. Most attacks happen in tropical waters, where shipwreck victims rarely survive. Danger zones include the coasts of North America, Japan, Australia, southern Asia, and Africa.

Shipwreck endurance record

Five fishermen from Costa Rica struggled in the immensity of the Pacific Ocean for an extraordinary 142 days, the longest such endurance on record. The ordeal began when a sudden storm overtook and sank the small fishing boat *Cairo III*.

Later they said that it was cooperation, perseverance, hope, and inner strength that saw them through their ordeal. When finally rescued, they had drifted 4,500 miles (7,240 km) from their home shores, crossing four time zones, and had survived on a diet of rainwater, fish and turtles.

One of the survivors said, "*La esperanza es lo último que se pierde*" ("Hope is the last thing you lose").

Extreme Facts

Waves the size of buildings

One in every 300,000 waves will exceed the average wave size by four times. So if you're sailing in seas 10 feet (3 meters) high, you've got a one in 300,000 chance of a monster wave of 40 feet (12 meters) — the size of a house — crashing down on you.

Amazing luck

Charles and Beryl Smeaton took three attempts to sail around Cape Horn in some of the most unpredictable waters in the world. During one attempt, a massive wave hit them from behind and flipped the boat over from end to end (pitch-poled). The wave was so powerful that Beryl's safety line was broken.

When the boat surfaced she was 160 feet (50 meters) away in huge seas and there was no way to rescue her. She was doomed.

Miraculously, the next monster wave plucked her up and deposited her back on the deck of the tiny boat. They all survived to tell the tale.

What do you think the chances of that happening were?

Crossing Raging Rivers

Have you ever thought about what you'd do if all
that stood between you and safety was a fast-run-
ning river? Any ideas? Make a raft, I hear you say.
Yes, good idea if you have the materials available.
Failing that, it's just down to you and your own
endeavors and resourcefulness. So here are a few
suggestions.

◆ **Pick your spot carefully**

Avoid crossing at wide sections or estuaries
unless you have a boat or raft. Head upstream
to find a safer spot. Don't cross where there are
high banks that are difficult to climb out on to,
and avoid obstructions in the water.

◆ **Check the current**

The current is likely to be at its fastest on the
outside of bends. Check the strength of current
before setting off by watching floating debris as
it goes by. Look out for obstructions which may
cause eddies and stoppers.[1]

◆ **Wading across**

The best surface for wading is gravel. Find a spot
where the water looks shallow. Use a stick to
help you balance and to test for hidden depths.
(I once went in up to my chest crossing a shallow river because I turned round to call a message to the man following me.)

[1]A stopper is a current that pulls you under the water and
keeps you pinned down.

Roll your pants up or take them off so they're dry for the other side. Keep boots or shoes on — they give a better grip than bare feet.

◆ **Swimming across**
This is definitely a last resort. If you must swim a river, even the strongest swimmer should use a flotation aid to save energy. It's amazing what you can find about the place: plastic bottles, logs, fuel cans all make good floats.

Alternatively, put your clothes in a waterproof bag, leaving plenty of air space. Then tie the neck, fold it over and tie it again. This makes a useful float that you can hold on to, using just your legs to get you across.

If you find yourself getting tangled up and hindered by weed in the water, change to crawl stroke (freestyle) to cut through it.

EXTREME

SURVIVAL TIP

Don't try swimming with trainers or shoes on — they'll drag you down.

Titanic

Leonardo di Caprio may not have survived in the film *Titanic*, but in real life, 707 people managed to survive the disaster.

The *Titanic* set off on its maiden voyage carrying 2,220 passengers from the docks of Southampton in early April 1912. While the great ship was speeding towards New York City, it struck an iceberg about 95 miles (153 km) south of the Grand Banks of Newfoundland, only minutes before midnight on April 14, 1912. The *Titanic* was swallowed by the sea in less than three hours. Many of the lifeboats carrying survivors were only half full because people panicked about overcrowding. (The boat had been designed with enough lifeboats for everyone on board, but because the boat deck looked too crowded, half of the lifeboats were taken off before they set sail!)

In the end, 1,513 passengers and crew perished in the freezing ocean water.

Swept Away by a Hurricane

Here is a story that illustrates the awesome power of the sea and the elements and also shows that the human spirit, although it may seem puny by comparison, can conquer in the end.

In October 1998, terrible floods hit Honduras and Nicaragua in Central America, caused by Hurricane Mitch in the Caribbean. A flood wave struck Laura Isabelle's house and sucked it and its inhabitants into the sea. Laura Isabelle managed to clamber up on the roof, holding her youngest child, but she was washed off into the sea and her child was wrenched from her arms. She was swept farther and farther away from shore. The sea was full of driftwood and debris from the hurricane. She managed to grab hold of a plank, and then clambered on to an uprooted tree.

Despite her desperation at having lost her family and her home, she clung to the tree with a fierce determination that the huge seas were not going to take her too. Laura Isabelle managed to pick up a pineapple and a coconut as they floated by and this gave her enough sustenance to keep going physically.

However, it was her strength of character that got her through her ordeal. At her lowest moments, she thought she might never be rescued but she sang songs to keep up her spirits and never gave in to those dark thoughts. After several days, a bird landed on her tree and she asked God to send the bird as a message to someone who might rescue her.

On her sixth day afloat in the vastness of the ocean, the British Royal Navy ship HMS *Sheffield* happened to see her clinging to her driftwood, and picked her up. She was saved, but she would still need her strength and determination to rebuild her life and her home.

Extreme Facts

In 1998, the El Niño ocean current warmed the Pacific, affecting weather patterns, and this led to devastating flooding in many parts of the globe. In Asia alone, an area the size of Europe was flooded, affecting over 300 million people.

Extreme Facts

In 1998, an estimated 3,000 people died in China owing to the extensive flooding. Over 240 million were affected, either by losing their crops and their livelihoods or by losing their homes and villages.

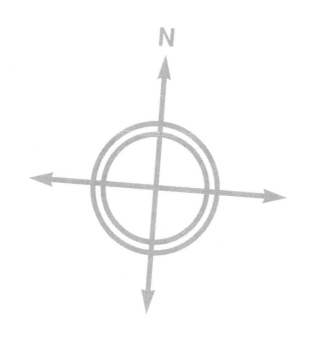

⟨ CHAPTER SEVEN ⟩

SURVIVING ANIMAL ATTACKS

I f you've ever had a dog on a leash come charging at you as you pass a stranger's house, you'll know what a fright it can give you. Imagine that multiplied by ten, and even that doesn't come close to what it is like to be rushed by a powerful ferocious, wild animal like a lion, tiger, bear, or rhinoceros.

Funnily enough, it's not the obvious killers like the big cats but the humble (but horribly bad-tempered) water buffalos that are responsible for killing most humans in India and Africa. They and the itsy-bitsy mosquito that carries the malaria virus responsible for millions of deaths in Third World countries.

Nevertheless, large predators do occasionally stumble across humans in the wilds, and if they attack, you have to be extremely resourceful to survive. Put yourself in the shoes of these survivors and work out what you'd have done if you'd found yourself in that situation.

Savaged by a Lion

In the 1960s, when big-game hunting was still allowed, a retired oil salesman from Honolulu with his wife and 14-year-old son went on safari in Tanzania. The hunter had laid a trap for a leopard — but they got more than they bargained for.

While inspecting the bait, the hunter and the wife came face to face with a hungry and very angry lion. It rushed at the man and woman as they stood in the bush. The hunter just managed to raise his rifle and shoot the lion as it charged, but it was only wounded. They ran for their lives and managed to make it back to the Land Rover.

They could hear the wounded animal growling and roaring in the bush, and the game hunter knew that he could not leave the animal in such pain. Not only that, but a wounded lion is an extremely dangerous one. So the hunter and his two African gun-bearers set off to track the lion and to put it out of its misery.

The Charge

By this time, the light was fading but they followed the blood until the tracker signaled that they were close. The lion lay panting under a big bush. One of the trackers raised his rifle to put an end to the lion's suffering. Unfortunately, the shot was poor and it only hit the lion's shoulder. The hunter raised his gun but the flash of the first shot in the dark had temporarily blinded him.

At that point, the lion charged. A quarter-ton of raging cat hit the hunter full length and knocked him flat. He was lying on his back with the lion on top of him. Its front legs were wrapped around him with its paws under his shoulderblades.

A Terrible Mauling

A lion often pauses for a second after his initial leap has knocked its victim down, and this one did just that. That tiny pause saved the hunter's life. He knew that within seconds the lion would bite him through the head.

He punched the lion in the nose with every ounce of strength he possessed, breaking the bones of his hand. The lion opened his mouth to growl and the hunter rammed his fist down its throat. Its teeth closed on his arm just below the elbow. Although he could feel the bones breaking in his arm, the hunter knew that as long as he kept his arm down the lion's gullet, it couldn't get at his head or throat.

The lion's claws were ripping at his back, and he brought his knees up to protect his vulnerable belly. Mercifully, his survival instincts had taken over and he was numb to the pain.

The lion shook the man like a ragdoll. The tracker managed to shoot it, but it took several shots to kill this hurt and angry beast.

SURVIVAL TIP

Mega-bites

We're not just talking lions here. Any bite from a wild animal, however small, can prove dangerous, mainly from infection.

If you're unlucky enough to get bitten, wash the area for at least five minutes to remove saliva. Then deal with the bleeding by dressing or bandaging. Even if the bite appears to heal, go and see a doctor once you're rescued.

Recovery

The hunter was in hospital for two months during which time the surgeons and doctors repaired his many wounds: two broken arms, a broken hand, a foot chewed and badly crushed, a horribly lacerated back, and a few deep holes in various parts of his body. But within three months, the hunter was back taking safaris and hunting other big cats again. He was either a sucker for punishment or a very brave man — what do you think?

It was the act of thrusting his hand down the lion's throat that probably saved this hunter. That's pretty cool thinking in a crisis, don't you think? Would you have have thought of it? Or would you have done things differently?

EXTREME

SURVIVAL TIP

Snake Bites

Try to avoid being bitten by seeing where you put your feet and giving snakes a chance to slither off when they hear you coming. Most poisonous snakes inject venom very deeply so the old myth about sucking out the poison is a bit of a waste of time. The best way to stop the poison spreading is:

◆ to make the victim relax (panic spreads the poison in the bloodstream round the body faster),

◆ put pressure on the wound site, and

◆ immobilize the affected part (keep it very, very still).

To apply the pressure, use a bandage (not a tourniquet, which can do more harm than good) above the bite and bandage down over it. So, for a bite above the ankle, start at the knee and work down. The bandage should be quite tight but not overly so – the limb shouldn't darken or swell up. A splint will stop the limb flexing. If possible, place the wound in cool water, or use ice to cool it. Try not to move the casualty. Keep a watchful eye on the casualty while you wait for help, and be ready to give artificial respiration.

Extreme Facts

Deadly Spiders

There are only a few spiders that are dangerous to humans, and most live in warmer parts of the world. Australia seems to have more than its fair share of poisonous spiders. There's the funnelweb and the redback, to name but two.

Extreme Facts

The famous black widow spider is responsible for several deaths a year in the USA, although only a small fraction of bites are fatal. Its venom is proportionally 15 times more potent than rattlesnake venom. Although the black widow accounts for roughly half of all spider bites reported annually in the USA, a human is no more likely to die from its bite than to be struck by lightning.

Bear Attack

While out walking in the woods, a 71-year-old farmer from Lake Michigan spotted a black bear who was lying in the dense thicket. Because of a heart condition he knew he could not outrun her so he started to walk as fast as he could back down the logging road. The bear came galloping up behind him and bit into his leg. She tried to pull him down but he knew that if that happened he was a goner, so he struggled to stand on his feet.

Fighting Back

Through his pain, the man managed to punch the bear hard on the nose. She let go of his leg and rose up on her hind feet. They then stood toe to toe and fought like two prize-fighters, except the bear had lethal claws. She kept clawing at his face and arms but the farmer kept fending her off by punching her around the nose and face, all the time backing away and trying to keep his arms up to protect his face.

He says that they continued fighting like this for nearly 20 minutes and never knew why the bear didn't finish him off with one powerful blow, as she easily could have done.

Striking It Lucky

As his last vestiges of strength started to ebb away, the farmer remembered the penknife in his pocket. He had to drop his guard to get it out and the bear raked his arm as he did so. He managed to open the knife and, with accurate aim plunged the penknife into the bear's eye. The bear lost all taste for the fight after that and, as quickly as she had come, she was gone. With his clothes hanging in ribbons and blood running from his face and arms, the old farmer

SURVIVAL TIP

If you're walking in a forest where there might be bears, make a non threatening noise as you go, so the bear can get its cubs out of your way. Humming or talking to yourself may also help to keep your spirits up.

managed to struggle back to his homestead. He was rushed to hospital, where he made a full recovery.

Would you have stood your ground and fought with the bear? Would you have remembered the knife? And used it?

Mind you, this is a very rare case because black bears don't usually pose a threat to humans. It's believed the bear must have had cubs and the unfortunate farmer wandered too close for this bear's liking.

Alligator Wrestling

An American showman used to put his head inside an alligator's mouth for the grand finale of his alligator-wrestling show. On one occasion during this act, a drop of sweat from the animal trainer's brow dropped on the alligator's tongue, triggering the reflex action that closed the alligator's jaws on his head.

The trainer's life flashed before his eyes as the grip tightened like a vice. Fellow trainers managed to get a large pole in between the animal's jaws and tried to pry them apart, but it took a long time and several men with sticks to free him. He suffered fractures and deep puncture wounds to the head.

Do you think he was brave, or asking for trouble?

EXTREME
SURVIVAL TIP

Run or Fight?

Many large and dangerous animals like rhinos, buffalos, and bears actually have very poor eyesight, relying on their sense of smell. So if you should come across one of these animals on your adventures, as long it hasn't got wind of you, you're best standing very still. If it sees you, slowly back off and talk in a calm, quiet manner. Don't make any sudden movements. Try to stay calm (easier said than done, I know) because animals can smell fear and an accident in your pants will definitely give you away.

If you can't bring yourself to freeze or if the animal gives chase, you'd better run as if your life depended on it – remembering to zigzag to confuse those with poor eyesight and those that charge in a straight line.

Shouting and making a great commotion may put off some predators. But climbing a tree should be a last resort – you could be up there quite some time. Anyway, it's not easy to climb when you're scared stiff.

Extreme Facts

The American alligator is a very close relative of the Nile crocodile. Both grow up to 18 feet (6 meters) in length and are able to kill and eat anything unlucky enough to stray into their path.

Alligators and crocodiles cannot chew, because their long, stabbing teeth don't have cutting or grinding edges. Instead, they simply rip off pieces of flesh and devour them whole.

Massively powerful, a crocodile can drag a full-grown zebra under water in just a few seconds. Many people are maimed or killed while collecting water at rivers and waterholes where the crocodiles lurk just beneath the surface of the water, waiting to snap up any creature that comes to drink.

Coping with Dogs

All dogs tend to conform to predictable rules of behavior. So, when you encounter a strange dog, the following tips may prove useful:

1. Look at how the dog approaches you.

◆ If it barks but stays put or backs off, it is probably too scared to attack.

◆ If it walks or runs towards you with its tail wagging in a low position, it's probably friendly and unlikely to bite.

◆ If it stiffens up, holds its tail high, snarls and stares at you, then be on your guard.

◆ If it shows its teeth, it may be safest to go no farther. But don't turn and run! Back away slowly.

2. Talk to dogs in a firm but quiet voice. If it approaches in a friendly way, stand still so that it can sniff you.

3. Never run past a strange dog, nor walk quickly away from it. This can make it chase you and you could get bitten as a result. Always walk or back away slowly if you feel the dog is threatening.

4. Try to avoid showing any fear. A dog can read fear in your eyes and body movements and can smell it. Keep calm, whistle (if you can), walk slowly, or speak firmly to the dog.

5. Never stare at a dog. Staring is a threat. A dog may read it as a challenge and attack you.

6. When delivery people or occasional visitors get bitten, it is usually as they are leaving a house. Remember it thinks you are an intruder. If in

doubt, back away slowly, keeping the dog in sight all the time.

Before you start carrying dog biscuits in your pockets or a big stick, it's worth remembering that dogs rarely attack. Most are scared of getting into a fight but like to act tough on their own territory.

CHAPTER EIGHT

Who can forget the scene in *The Great Escape* when Steve McQueen tries to jump the prisoner-of-war camp perimeter fence on his motorbike? What do you mean, you've never seen it? It's one of my favorite films, all about . . . well, enough of that. Get it out on video. It's great.

But really, escaping from captors may have been glamorized by Hollywood, but the acts of courage of these real-life survivors are true enough.

Behind Enemy Lines

In the autumn of 1990, Iraq invaded Kuwait. The international community were outraged by this act of aggression and vowed to do something about it. So started the Gulf War.

On the night of January 22, 1991, at a remote airfield in Saudi Arabia, under cover of darkness and in the utmost secrecy, eight members of the British SAS regiment boarded a helicopter that was to infiltrate them deep behind enemy lines. Their mission, under the command of Sergeant Andy McNab, was to sever the underground communication link between Baghdad and northwest Iraq, and to seek and destroy mobile Scud launchers before Israel was provoked into entering the war. Their radio call sign was Bravo Two-Zero. This mission became one of the most famous stories of courage and survival in modern warfare and the patrol is the most highly decorated in British history since the Boer War in the late nineteenth century.

Each member of the patrol was laden with a mighty 210 lb (95 kg) of equipment. Just imagine walking anywhere carrying that lot! In fact, they traveled 20 miles (32 km) across flat desert to reach their objective and find a hiding place before first light. By late evening of January 24, the patrol was spotted deep behind enemy lines. The Iraqis attacked with armor. After a fierce firefight, the patrol escaped. They decided to head for the Syrian border, 120 miles (192 km) to the northwest.

Escape Across the Desert

That first night, in pitch darkness and with weather cold enough to freeze diesel fuel, they covered 53 miles (85 km) — that's more than two marathons! Nothing had prepared them for the vicious cold of the desert winter and they began to suffer from hypothermia. The members of the patrol got separated from one another. Four men were captured and three died. Only one, Chris Ryan, escaped — but in their wake lay 150 Iraqi dead and wounded.

Left on his own, Chris Ryan beat off another Iraqi attack and kept going. Traveling at night, he narrowly avoided detection by the Iraqi villagers. He had to cope with searing heat during the day and freezing temperatures at night. Eventually he made it to Syria and from there was flown home to recover. He had weighed 176 lb (80 kg) when he left Saudi Arabia at the start of the mission, but ten days later, when he reached Syria, he'd lost 36 lb (16 kg).

For his escape, Chris Ryan was awarded the Military Medal.

Torture

Meanwhile, the four who had been captured were delivered to Baghdad, where three of them were savagely tortured. It took physical and mental toughness to survive their tormentors — and their intensive SAS training went partway to helping them

Extreme Facts

The SAS motto is "Who Dares Wins."

Extreme Facts

Name, rank and number

Special-forces troops are trained in interrogation techniques and ways in which to withstand them. Under the Geneva Convention (the internationally agreed rules for warfare), the only information that a captured member of the armed forces has to divulge is his or her name, rank and military number. However, captors rarely settle for so little information.

An injection of a "truth drug" (a chemical compound which overcomes the subject's conscious resistance) may be used to make a prisoner divulge secret information. It is almost impossible to withstand the disabling effects of this drug. However, it is not widely available, and more brutal ways of extracting vital information are often employed.

overcome their ordeal. After the war, they were handed over by the Iraqis and returned to the UK.

This type of special-forces soldiering relies on enormous courage, endurance, dark humor, and self-belief in the face of overwhelming odds.

SURVIVAL TIP

Torture Tactics

◆ Your oppressors want to build a relationship with you so that you start to trust them and are then more likely to spill the beans. So they may offer you drinks, food, chocolate, cigarettes, etc. Don't be fooled.

◆ Once you break from the formula of name, rank, and number, it is very difficult to stop. The information just comes spilling out. So stick to your guns.

◆ If you do say more than name, rank, and number, however innocent your words, the enemy can cut and edit your conversation and broadcast your words with a completely different meaning. This is purely propaganda but it can be very distressing for loved ones at home.

◆ They will try to disorient you and make you feel uncomfortable by making you sit or stand in strange positions, making you very hot and then very cold, light and then dark – all in an effort to weaken your resistance.

◆ Your watch will be taken from you and you will have no idea of the time. You will not even be aware of the changes in day and night because you'll be kept in artificial light. This is very disorienting and your captivity can feel like months when it's actually only days.

◆ Never forget that once your oppressors believe they know all that you know, you are expendable. So stick to name, rank, and number.

EXTREME
SURVIVAL TIP

Escape and Evasion

When you are trying to pass through countryside undetected, you should take off any brightly-colored clothing and discard it or hide it under darker clothes. Smear your face and hands with mud and dirt (this is the basic principle behind camouflage cream as used by the military) so that you are harder to detect among the foliage. And remember, once camouflaged, if you stay still, you will be very hard to spot, even if an enemy is looking right at you, as long as they don't know for sure where you are.

The Colditz Story

Probably the most famous escape and survival stories come from the Second World War. The Colditz story may be the most legendary of them all.

Colditz was an impregnable German castle from which no one had escaped in the 1914-18 First World War. It was where the Germans kept the really "bad boys" in the Second World War — those who had tried to escape several times before from other POW camps. The guards outnumbered the prisoners at all times and the castle was floodlit at night from every angle, despite the blackout. There were clear drops of 100 feet (30 meters) or so on the outside of barred windows, and sentries all around the camp within a perimeter of barbed wire.

But the Germans overlooked the fact that in Colditz they had accumulated all the best escape technicians of the Allied forces under one roof. And morale could not have been higher.

Daring escape attempts took place all the time, although most were thwarted, resulting in long periods of solitary confinement for those who were caught. It did not deter the prisoners — they tried to escape time and time again. Could you have kept trying to break out, knowing the consequences? Solitary confinement is no fun and for some, the price was even higher — they were shot as they tried to escape.

For many, the hardest part of their escape was crossing enemy country to neutral territory. They never knew when they might be detected or when someone might betray their whereabouts. Just imagine living as a fugitive with that sort of stress to contend with!

By the time the camp was relieved by the Americans, on April 15, 1945, only five British officers had successfully managed to escape and make it back home, along with a handful of other Allied prisoners of various nationalities. All showed phenomenal courage and determination.

Across the Roofs

One of the legendary Colditz escapees was Pat Reid. He was first caught by the Germans in May 1940. After several attempts at escaping from

POW camps, he was transferred to Colditz where he eventually made his successful "home run" in October 1942.

He and three other Brits managed to make a sortie out of the windows of the camp kitchens, over the low roofs of various store buildings and into the adjoining German Kommandatur [commander's office] courtyard.

Then, dropping to the ground, they had to cross the path of a sentry when his back was turned, and crawl across the dimly lit area in front of the Kommandatur to a small open pit in the far corner of the courtyard.

Unseen, they slipped into a cellar and then squeezed up and out of a tight chimney flue [bending a bar at the top to get out] to find themselves on the moat side of the castle. They used knotted sheets to drop down the 18 feet (5.5 meters) of the moat. Silently, they crept past the barracks where the guards slept and reached the final hurdle — the outer wall. It was only 10 feet (3 meters) high, with coils of barbed wire stretched along the top, and they all got over without harm.

Fugitives in Enemy Territory

At this point, the foursome split into two groups for the long journey through enemy territory to neutral Switzerland. Pat Reid and Hank Wardle used forged papers and civilian clothing to travel the 400 miles (640 km) to the border by train. They were frequently challenged and it took nerves of steel to mingle with their enemy in this way. When asked, they passed themselves off as Flemish workers, which accounted for their unusual accent when speaking German. They were challenged many times but their nerve held.

Finally, they left the railway and set off across country by foot to reach the border. Their progress was compromised several times by farm workers but they always managed to dodge back into the woods and make a detour to get away. Skirting armed sentries and hostile villages, after two days of walking, they crossed into Switzerland. Amazingly, the other two crossed the frontier safely the following night.

Careful planning, good team work, and an ability to think on their feet were essential for the success of this scheme.

EXTREME SURVIVAL TIP

Losing the trail

Prison guards and police forces often use dogs in pursuit of escaping prisoners because of their excellent sense of smell. If men with dogs are hunting you, make for water and wade through the stream or river to put the dogs off your scent. This will buy you time but the dogs will patrol the banks until they pick up your trail again where you exit the water.

EXTREME
SURVIVAL TIP

On the Run

When you have to go to the toilet (let's face it, with a pack of dogs bearing down on you who can resist the urge?), make sure you cover your faeces with dirt. A fresh pile of poop is a telltale sign that you've passed this way and also gives an indication of what sort of lead you've got over your pursuers.

Extreme Facts

The world record for the longest-running escape belongs to Leonard T. Fristoe, who escaped from Nevada State Prison on December 15, 1923. He was turned in by his son and recaptured on November 15, 1969 at the age of 77 in California. He had survived 46 years without detection under the name of Claude Willis. He was originally sentenced for killing two sheriff's deputies in the 1920s.

On the right track

In the latter days of the war, the entire Dutch contingent was herded into a train to be taken from Colditz to another POW camp. En route, they unhitched their railway carriage and as it came to a standstill they all escaped in various directions. I bet their German guards were hopping mad, don't you?

Civilians at War

You don't have to be in the military, in the police force, or a criminal to deal with an enemy. There are conflicts all over the world where innocent civilians are caught up or deliberately attacked.

Violence between ethnic groups and civil wars in such places as Bosnia and Sudan have made many families homeless. They have been forced to make long journeys across hostile country to find a safe haven. It's hard to imagine your neighbor turning you out of your own home and threatening your life if you don't leave the area, but this is what has happened to thousands of families in such areas of civil conflict.

Could you see yourself taking the few items you can carry and traveling the length of the country on foot in order to reach safety? The worry of an uncertain future alone is enough to wear you out, let alone the physical hardship. It does not bear thinking about. But refugees need survival skills just as much as adventurers do.

⟨◦ CHAPTER NINE ◦⟩

How many times have you watched a film and said during a nail-biting chase, "Don't climb up there, there's no escape" or, during a war film, "Wait for covering fire — don't stand up . . .Oh, another one bites the dust."

Basically, we all think we know best. But, believe me, it's much easier being wise while sitting in the comfort of your home than it is to make the right decisions when you're out there facing danger.

But if you're so sure that you know what you're doing, give these survival scenarios a bash and see how you get on. You decide how you would handle the situation and why. By the way, there is often no right or wrong answer in these situations — you simply have to do what you think is right at the time.

However, at the end of the chapter, I will give you an outline of what I would do in the same situation and my reasons, just for interest's sake. Don't worry if our answers aren't the same — who's to say who is right and who is wrong until you're faced with the real thing?

1. Towering Inferno

You and your little brother are trapped upstairs and your house is on fire. You cannot reach the phone and the stairs are cut off by fierce flames. Smoke is starting to come up to where you are. Time is running out. What do you do?

2. Stranded

There are four of you in the party and you've been walking all day in the hills. It's late in the afternoon and a boy in your group has fallen and badly twisted his ankle. It's swelling and he's unable to walk on it. Bad weather has closed in: freezing rain and low cloud give poor visibility. You have no food left but have got bivvy bags and a map. What do you do next?

3. Ice Maiden

While out walking the dog on a cold winter's day, you hear cries for help. You follow the sound down a wooded bank until you see a young girl who has fallen through the ice on the river about six feet from the bank. She can't get out and is weakening very quickly in the icy waters. How can you help?

4. Lost in a Strange City

You have become separated from your school party and find yourself alone in a large, unfamiliar city. You have some money with you but it's only large-denomination notes. You do not know the address of where you are staying. Get out of that one!

5. Plane Crash

Your twelve-seater plane goes down in the middle of the Amazon jungle. Everyone except the pilot survives the crash but the radio is destroyed by the crash landing. Where do you go from here?

6. War Zone

You are a soldier and your unit is being inserted into a war zone under cover of darkness. You all know that the first person out of the helicopter may very well get injured, if not killed. Whom do you send?

◆ The old experienced sergeant
◆ The young officer who should lead from the front
◆ The young, inexperienced recruit
◆ The sharp, street-wise lance-corporal who is very keen

You decide who should jump out first. This is a good brainteaser to share with your friends because you can discuss it till the cows come home.

My Suggestions

Don't forget what I said — this is what I would do in the above situations but it doesn't mean that what you came up with is wrong if it differs from my answers. Just think about my reasoning and see if it can improve upon your plan or not.

1. Towering Inferno

First, open a window on to the street and try to attract attention so that someone can call the emergency services. If you are successful, close the door of the room, seal the bottom with a towel or clothing, and wait for the fire service, all the time comforting and reassuring your little brother.

If you have no windows that open, find a heavy object and, with your brother safely behind you, break a window in the bottom corner.

If there is no help available and the fire is getting dangerously close, think whether there is a window that opens onto a flat roof, such as a porch. Again, seal the room and then climb out on the flat roof, helping your brother out after you. Shout for help.

If there are no flat roofs, then throw bedding or soft furnishings out of the window and lower your brother as far as you can, feet first, out of the window and let him drop down on the soft cushioning below. Ask him to move out of your way and then lower yourself out of the window so that you are at full stretch before you let go, feet first. Here's to soft landings!

2. Stranded

My first decision would be whether we could carry the casualty out or not. If that proved impossible, then I would send the two strongest members of the team for help. The third person would stay and look after the casualty.

The two going for help should study the map before setting off to find the nearest telephone or civilization, such as a bar, restaurant, or house, all of which are marked on large-scale maps. They should leave extra warm clothing, etc. for the casualty and his carer. Make sure they know the location of the casualty and friend so they can direct the rescue party to find them.

If you're not sure of where you are on the map, then remember the details of your descent so that you can tell the rescuers from where and how far you've come. Give the rescuers full details of the injury before they set off, and tell them at what time it happened.

3. Ice Maiden

Do not under any circumstances go out on the ice. If she went through, there's every chance that you will too. Instead, hold on to a tree or strong branch or tie yourself securely to it with a scarf or belt. Using anything that comes to hand, such as the dog's lead, a scarf, belt, or a strong branch, throw it to the girl (still holding on to one end, of course). Once she has caught hold of the other end, she can hold on and you can help pull her to safety.

All the time this rescue is going on, keep calling for help so that if you attract someone's attention, they can go for the emergency services. Unless your dog is trained to the standard of Lassie, keep him well out of the way.

4. Lost in a Strange City

Don't just go up to the first person you see. Find a police officer or police station and give them your details and the details of your school.

If you can't find any police, go to a large, familiar chain store or well-known fast-food outlet

EXTREME

SURVIVAL TIP

If you're dumb or unlucky enough to find yourself on ice and it starts to crack, lie down. This spreads the weight and like this you can inch your way back to safety. Putting all your weight through one foot as you run towards solid ground exerts enormous force on the ice and is likely to send you crashing through into the icy waters below.

such as McDonald's and get change for the phone. Phone your school and get details of where you are staying and let them know what has happened and your whereabouts. If you can't get any change but have found a public phone, call the operator and reverse the charges, again calling the school. If you

EXTREME

SURVIVAL TIP

Major railway stations usually have maps of the city.

have a contact in the city, call him or her.

Stay in a heavily populated area — don't go wandering off the beaten track or into dark back streets. Keep warm. The shop or restaurant will understand the situation and let you wait inside for your rescuers.

Next time, make sure you have the address of where you are staying and the telephone number and, if possible, your teacher's mobile phone number, if he or she has got one.

5. Plane Crash

Basically, you must stay by the plane because that is what the search party will be looking for. However, since you are quite a large group, you can pool your resources. Split into small groups and send out a search party to scout around and for food collection. They should follow a structured pattern, traveling for a set time and in a set direction, so that you know roughly where they are if help arrives.

Find signaling and communication materials such as flares, mirrors, and mobile phones. Check out what specialist skills the passengers have — medical knowledge may be useful, and if there's an electrician on board, perhaps he or she could have a go at mending the radio. Work out a plan of action for when a search plane is seen nearby or overhead, so that you can make the best use of fires, flares, mirrors, signaling and so on.

You should also think about a survival strategy in case it turns into a long stay, bearing in mind the basic requirements of food, shelter, and warmth.

Finally, don't forget to use what is at hand before you start rooting about in the jungle. Search the plane for useful materials such as blankets and food, and search the luggage — you'll be amazed how many useful things you may find.

6. War Zone

This is a bit of a trick question really. It's used in officer selection for certain elite regiments. The answer is that the person nearest the door should be first out of the helicopter, otherwise there will be chaos inside the chopper.

Did anyone get that answer? Well done if you did! Believe me, it's foxed many young hopefuls wanting to be promoted.

The lesson to take from this is that planning is very important, of course, but in the long run, never let elaborate theories stand in the way of common sense. That's the best survival tool of all.

CHAPTER TEN

Sometimes your survival instinct is at its strongest when you see someone else in difficulty. It's a natural reaction to want to help and your quick thinking and cool reactions can save lives. But remember that a dead hero is no good to anyone — so never put your life in danger to rescue a person or an animal. If it's too dangerous for you to risk helping yourself, then put all your efforts into getting the rescue services so they can come and use their specialist equipment and knowledge.

That said, there are times when a little bit of basic first-aid know-how can make all the difference. So here are a few life-saving tricks of the trade used by voluntary services around the world.

In an Emergency

If you ever find yourself in a situation where a

friend or a stranger is in need of first aid, there are three crucial steps to take.

Step One

DON'T rush in.

Assess the situation and make sure that you are not putting yourself at risk if you help. Once you've made sure that you and the casualty are safe from further harm, you can turn your mind to medical attention.

Step Two

What condition is the casualty in?

Check whether the casualty is unconscious by gently shaking them and asking questions loudly like "What happened?" or give commands such as "Open your eyes." You can ask anything you like really — "Do you like hamburgers? " will do. Then check whether they're breathing? Are they injured? Is the condition due to injury or drowning?

If someone is with you, send them for help and to pass on details of the casualty's condition.

Step Three

Take action.

If it's an obvious injury, treat the casualty (see examples below) and then call for an ambulance, if necessary.

If the person is not breathing, carry out the following resuscitation sequence for one minute before calling an ambulance. Then carry on if the person is still not breathing.

Artificial Respiration

If the casualty is not breathing:

1. Gently tilt the head well back, making sure there are no obvious obstructions in the mouth and that the tongue is not blocking the airways. Then watch and listen for up to ten seconds to see if there is any breathing (you might see some slight chest movement, or hear gentle sounds of breathing, or even feel the breath on your cheek).

2. If there is no sign of breathing, pinch the casualty's nose quite firmly so no air can escape that way.

3. Take a full breath and, placing your lips over their mouth to make a good seal, blow out until you see their chest rise. It takes about two seconds for full inflation on an adult — less for a child.

4. Let the chest fall and then repeat mouth-to-mouth again. Check for signs of recovery.

If breathing returns, put the casualty in the recovery position. If not, carry on with mouth-to-mouth and remember to stay calm — you're doing the right thing.

The Recovery Position

This is the safest position for someone needing medical attention.

1. Kneel by the casualty's side and straighten their arms and legs. Tuck their hand nearest to you (arm straight and palm upward) under their thigh.

2. Bring the arm farthest away from you across their chest. Put their hand, palm outwards, against their cheek and, using your other hand, pull up the casualty's far leg, just above the knee.

3. Keeping the casualty's hand pressed against their cheek, pull on the far leg and roll the casualty towards you, until they are lying on their side, head resting on their hand.

4. Don't let the casualty roll too far forwards. Bend their upper leg at the knee so that it is at right angles to the body. This stops them rolling forwards.

5. Make sure that the casualty's head is tilted well back to keep the airways open. Also check that their lower arm is lying free alongside their back with palm facing upwards.

Sounds complicated, doesn't it? Actually, it's much easier to do than it sounds. So give it a try at home with a friend. Practice until putting someone in the recovery position becomes second nature to you. Then, if you need to use it in an emergency, you'll have no problems.

Nasty Injuries

Do you go weak at the knees at the sight of blood? Well, don't worry. I've known hard-bitten war heroes who feel faint when they see a drop of the red stuff. But the important thing is that they overcome their fear to help others, and so can you.

Severe Bleeding

If you come across somebody who has had an accident and is bleeding heavily, you have to act quickly.

1. Remove or cut the casualty's clothing to expose the wound and then, using a pad (sterile if possible but I've never had one on hand), cover the wound. Press firmly on the pad with your fingers or the palm of your hand.

2. Lay the casualty down and keep the bleeding bit above the level of their heart.

3. Apply a sterile dressing (if available) over the original pad and bandage firmly in place. Don't worry if blood seeps through, just bandage another pad on top but make sure it's not too tight — check it at intervals and loosen if necessary.

4. Ring for an ambulance, giving details of where the injury is and how severe the bleeding is when you call.

5. Treat for shock (see below); check breathing, pulse, and level of response regularly (but don't keep pestering them — once every 10 minutes is enough).

SURVIVAL TIP

◆ Don't apply a tourniquet.

◆ If the casualty passes out, place them in the recovery position and be ready to resuscitate if necessary.

◆ Wear gloves if possible to protect against infection.

Shock

It's amazing how tough some people are. They can survive the most horrific injuries, yet the shock of an accident or unexpected event can put them out of action. In fact, shock can kill a casualty as easily as the wounds. So keep a watchful eye on them.

1. Lay the casualty down and raise their legs as high as possible (within reason please — you don't want them doing a head stand!)

2. Loosen tight clothing, particularly around the neck, chest, and waist.

3. Call for an ambulance, explaining that the casualty is in shock.

4. Monitor breathing and pulse and level of response by asking simple questions ("What's your name?" will do) every ten minutes.

EXTREME

SURVIVAL TIP

Signs of shock to look out for:
- A racing pulse
- Gray-blue skin, especially on lips
- Sweaty and cold, clammy skin

Later:
- Weakness or giddiness
- Nausea or thirst
- Quick, light breathing
- A weak pulse

Eventually:
- Restlessness
- Gasping for air
- Unconsciousness
- Cardiac arrest

Head Injury

These often look a lot worse than they really are but it's very alarming for someone to have blood pouring down his or her face. It's up to you to stay calm and to reassure the patient. Then get to work!

1. Control the bleeding by putting a clean pad over the wound and pressing on it firmly, remembering to replace any flaps of skin that are out of place first. (Can you believe the things you have to do?)

2. Secure the dressing with a bandage.

3. Lay the casualty down, keeping their head and shoulders slightly raised on a makeshift pillow. Check that the casualty is comfortable.

4. Take or send the casualty to hospital.

EXTREME

SURVIVAL TIP

◆ If the casualty falls unconscious, put them in the recovery position and be ready to resuscitate if necessary.

◆ If the bleeding doesn't stop, press firmly on the wound again and put another pad on top of the first.

Broken Bones

If someone has had a bad or awkward fall, he or she may well break a bone that will need setting in hospital. In the meantime, you can help.

1. Support the affected part of the body above and below the fracture, perhaps resting it on padding (something like a towel or cushion), and keep it steady in a comfortable position.

2. Call for an ambulance or go with the casualty to hospital.

EXTREME
SURVIVAL TIP

◆ Don't try to bandage a broken bone if medical help is on the way.

◆ Don't move the broken limb unnecessarily.

◆ Don't give a casualty with a suspected fracture, anything to eat or drink.

SAVING LIVES

Burns

Whether it's from fire or from scalding liquids, a burn is a particularly nasty injury and your quick actions can definitely make a difference to the after-effects of a burn.

1. Cool the burn down by pouring cold liquid over it or holding it under running water for at least ten minutes.

2. Remove any restrictions such as clothing or jewelry from the burn area before it starts to swell.

3. Cover the burn and surrounding area with a sterile dressing or, failing that, a clean piece of material.

4. If the burn is large or deep, treat the casualty for shock (see above).

5. Call for an ambulance or go with the casualty to hospital.

EXTREME SURVIVAL TIP

- ◆ Don't apply lotions, ointment, or butter to a burn.

- ◆ Try not to touch the injured area and don't burst any blisters.

- ◆ Never remove anything sticking to the burn.

With any luck, you'll never have to use these skills, but, when you're out adventuring, it's surprising how many times you run across people who need your help. First-aid skills are good skills to have. They've got me and my friends out of difficulties on many occasions. How about you?

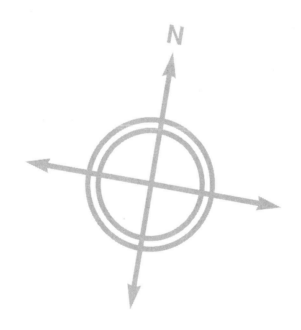

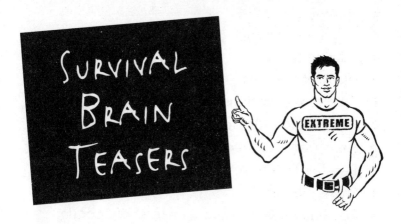

CHAPTER ELEVEN

SURVIVAL BRAIN TEASERS

Training experts around the world, whether it be the military, outdoor-education specialists, or the emergency services, use the following exercises or variations on them, to test the knowledge of their recruits. Let's see how you get along, shall we?

1 Adrift in the Ocean

There has been a severe fire on your boat. You and the three other crew members managed to make it into a life raft unharmed, but most of your supplies have been destroyed. You are floating helplessly in the middle of the ocean. The only things that you've managed to salvage undamaged after the fire are:

- Fishing gear
- 5-gallon can of water
- Sextant
- Mosquito netting
- Shaving mirror
- Maps of the area
- One case of rations
- Seat cushion (flotation device)
- Small transistor radio, receiving only
- 2-gallon (9-liter) can of oil / gas mixture
- Shark repellent
- 20 square feet (2 square meters) of opaque plastic
- One and a half pints (approx. 1 liter) of strong rum
- 15 feet (4.5 meters) of nylon rope
- 2 boxes of chocolate bars

In the first column of the table on the next page, number the items from one to fifteen in descending order of importance. For example, if you think the radio is the most important item, put a one in the box next to it. And if the next most important is the fishing gear, put a two in the box next to fishing gear and so on.

When you have completed the exercise, read on to find out the experts' order and their reasoning.

Undamaged Items	Your order	Experts' order	Difference
Fishing gear			
5-gallon can of water			
sextant			
mosquito netting			
Shaving mirror			
Maps of the area			
One case of rations			
Seat cushion (flotation device)			
Small transistor radio — receiving only			
2-gallon can of oil/gas mixture			
Shark repellent			
20 square feet of opaque plastic			
1½ pints of rum			
15 feet of nylon rope			
2 boxes of chocolate bars			
TOTAL			

Answers:

Correct Number	Reason
1. Shaving mirror	Vital for signaling air-sea rescue.
2. 2-gallon can oil/gas mixture	Vital for signaling. The mixture would float and could be ignited (when raft is clear of it, obviously).
3. 5-gallon can of water	Necessary to replenish loss by perspiring.
4. One case of rations	Provides basic food.
5. 20 square feet of opaque plastic	To collect rainwater and provide shelter.
6. 2 boxes of chocolate bars	A reserve food supply.
7. Fishing gear	Ranked lower than chocolate bars because a bird in the hand is worth two in the bush. There's no guarantee you'll catch any fish.
8. 15 feet of nylon rope	Can be used to secure equipment to prevent it from falling overboard.
9. Seat cushion (flotation device)	A lifesaver if someone falls overboard.
10. Shark repellent	Obvious.
11. 1½ pints of rum	Contains enough alcohol to serve as antiseptic for injuries, of little value otherwise. Will cause dehydration if drunk.
12. Small transistor radio	No transmitting capabilities but will keep survivors entertained.
13. Maps of the area	Worthless without navigational aids. It does not really matter where you are but where the rescuers are.
14. Mosquito netting	There are no mosquitoes at sea.
15. Sextant	Relatively useless without tables and chronometer.

According to the experts, the basic supplies needed when a person is stranded in mid-ocean are articles to attract attention and articles to aid survival until the rescuers arrive. The basic reason for ranking signaling devices above life-sustaining items (food and water) is that if you cannot signal, there is almost no chance of being spotted and rescued. Most rescues occur during the first 36 hours and you can survive that long without food and water.

Articles for navigation are of little importance. Even if a small life raft were capable of reaching land, it would be impossible to store enough food and water to subsist during that period of time. So, of primary importance are the shaving mirror and the two-gallon can of oil/gas mixture. These items could be used for signaling the air-sea rescue. Of secondary importance are items such as water and food.

Compare your ratings with the experts'

Now fill in the table with the experts' order and then work out the difference, as in the following example, in order to get your score.

Undamaged Items	Your order	Experts' order	Difference
Fishing gear	5	7	2
5-gallon can of water	1	3	2
Sextant	7	15	8
Mosquito netting	14	14	-
Shaving mirror	2	1	1
Maps of area	11	13	2
One case of rations	6	4	2
. . . and so on			

Now add up the difference column to check how well you've scored.

DIFFERENCE TOTAL

0–20: Excellent — you'll be rescued within 24 hours.

21–30: Good — rescue within 36 hours. You're thirsty and need a shower.

31–40: Average — rescue within 60 hours. You're hungry, thirsty, and smelly.

41–50: Fair — rescue within 84 hours. You're sucking fish juice and looking hungrily at fellow raft mates.

Over 50: Poor — you're shark bait.

2 Lost In Space

Now you're getting the hang of it, why not try this NASA exercise, allegedly devised by the space-exploration experts themselves?

You are a member of a space crew scheduled to rendezvous with a mother ship on the lighted surface of the moon. Because of mechanical difficulties, your ship was forced to land at a spot some 200 miles (320 km) from the rendezvous point. During landing much of the equipment was damaged. Your survival depends on reaching the mother ship, and you're going to have to walk. What will you carry?

Below are listed the fifteen items left intact and undamaged after the landing. Your task is to arrange them in order of importance to your crew in allowing them to reach the mother ship. Place 1 by the most important item, then 2 and so on up to number 15 — the least important item.

Give yourself five minutes to attempt this exercise . . . and good luck!

◆ Box of matches
◆ Food concentrate
◆ 50 feet (4.5 meters) of nylon rope
◆ Parachute silk
◆ Portable heating unit
◆ Two .45 pistols
◆ One case of dehydrated pet milk
◆ Two 100 lb (45 kg) tanks of oxygen
◆ Stellar maps
◆ Life raft
◆ Magnetic compass
◆ 5 gallons of water (approx. 20 liters)
◆ Signal flares
◆ First aid kit with injection needles
◆ Solar-powered FM receiver-transmitter

When you've finished, look below at the NASA experts' ratings. Fill in the table with their ranking and work out the difference in scores. You'll then get a grading for how well you completed this exercise.

Undamaged Items	Your order	Experts' order	Difference
Box of matches			
Food concentrate			
50 feet (4.5 meters) of nylon rope			
Parachute silk			
Portable heating unit			
Two .45 pistols			
One case of dehydrated pet milk			
Two 100 lb (45 kg) tanks of oxygen			
Stellar maps			
Life raft			
Magnetic compass			
5 gallons of water (approx. 20 liters)			
Signal flares			
First aid kit with injection needles			
Solar-powered FM receiver-transmitter			
TOTAL			

Answers

Correct number	Reason
1. Two 100 lb oxygen tanks	Oxygen is the most pressing need. Because the gravitational pull of the moon is only one-sixth of what it is here on earth, these tanks would weigh only about 30 lb (13.5 kg).
2. 5 gallons of water	You get up to 200°+ temperatures on the moon's lighted surface. You would have a pressing need for water to replenish fluid loss.
3. Stellar maps	NASA saw this as the most important single means of navigation.
4. Food concentrate	This would be very nutritious and food would be one of your concerns.
5. Solar-powered FM receiver-transmitter	This could be used as a distress-signal transmitter and for possible communication with the mother ship.
6. 50 feet of nylon rope	It has a number of uses — tying people together when climbing small mountains, tying all the equipment together and pulling it.
7. First aid kit	The ampoules of injection medicine may be valuable.
8. Parachute silk	This is ideal protection from the sun's rays. Remember, you're on the lighted side of the moon.

9. Life raft

This has a variety of uses. Inflated it gives protection from the sun and is a means of carrying injured people or equipment. NASA favored using the CO_2 bottles on the raft for propulsion across chasms, etc.

10. Signal flares

Probably useful if you could get close enough to the ship for them to be seen.

11. Two .45 pistols

NASA says that self-propulsion devices could be made from these.

12. Once case of dehydrated pet milk

This would have some usefulness as food mixed a little at a time with food concentrate, if available.

13. Portable heating unit

This would be useful only if you landed on the dark side of the moon.

14. Magnetic compass

If there is a magnetic field on the moon, it doesn't seem to be polarized. The needle would probably spin and be of little use.

15. Box of matches

Since there is little atmosphere on the moon, the matches wouldn't burn. So they have little or no use.

Now add up the difference column to check how well you've scored.

Under 20: Excellent — you'll reach the mother ship without delay.

20–30: Good — you'll get there but it will take some time.

31–40: Average — you make it but you'll be exhausted and very hungry and thirsty.

41–50: Fair — you get close but don't reach the ship. You have to send off flares to be rescued. A close shave.

Over 50: Poor — wave bye-bye to Earth. The mother ship has gone.

3 Desert Air Crash

Your plane develops mechanical difficulties and crashes in the middle of the Sinai Desert, Egypt, close to a war zone. The wreckage is scattered over a large area but you and your three fellow survivors manage to recover the following items intact. Choose the six most important and useful items that you can use as a crash survivor in descending order of importance.

Materials salvaged from the crash:

◆ Salt tablets
◆ Crate of mineral water, enough for nearly 2 pints (1 liter) each
◆ Book: Edible Wildlife of the Sinai
◆ Various sunglasses — enough for a pair each
◆ 3.5 pints (2 liters) of whisky
◆ An overcoat each
◆ Shaving mirror
◆ Flashlight
◆ Machete (jungle knife)
◆ Survey map of Sinai
◆ Large plastic raincoat
◆ Orienteering compass
◆ First-aid box (assorted bandages)
◆ Revolver (loaded)
◆ Bright-red parachute
◆ 4 tubes of extra strong mints
◆ Suntan lotion (nonscreening)

MY TOP SIX	
1	
2	
3	
4	
5	
6	

Once you've completed your answers, see below what the experts think.

Answers

Item	Score for each item in top six	
Shaving mirror	10	Useful as signaling device.
An overcoat each	9	Useful for cold nights.
Crate of mineral water	8	Essential to replace lost fluids during hot days.
Flashlight	7	Useful signaling device.
Bright-red parachute	6	Good protection from sun during day and also as signaling device.
Machete	5	Handy tool and weapon.
Large plastic raincoat	3	Useful for collecting condensation in the morning and protection/warmth at night.
Revolver	3	Signaling and self-defence.
Sunglasses	3	To protect eyes in blazing sunlight.
First-aid box	3	Obvious.
Orienteering compass	2	Useful in conjunction with maps if decide to leave wreckage.
Survey map of Sinai	2	As above.
Book	2	Useful if not rescued for some time.
Extra strong mints	1	Minimal energy value. Might take the nasty taste in your mouth away temporarily.

117
EXTREME
SURVIVAL GUIDE

Suntan lotion	1	Nonscreening so provides no protection. A good tan should be the last thing on your mind.
Whisky	1	Alcohol dehydrates so it would be disastrous to drink it. Could possibly be used as antiseptic for injuries.
Salt tablets	1	No real value in the desert.

TOTAL SCORE

40–45: Excellent – you stand a good chance of being rescued and of surviving in relative comfort.

31–39: Good – you'll be rescued after a few days, feeling a little the worse for wear.

15–30: Fair – you're going to be extremely thirsty, sun-burned, and near exhaustion before you're rescued, but you should survive – just!

Under 15: Poor – sorry! The desert is an unforgiving place and I don't think you're going to make it.

CHAPTER TWELVE

Between us, we've come a long way since that early assessment of your survival knowledge. I don't know about you but I'm feeling a bit whacked. How about we sit down, put our feet up, and try this quiz to see how much you've learned along the way?

Just about all the topics covered have been touched upon in the book so, if you're struggling, you can always go back and reread the bit that relates to that particular question.

Right then, get your survival hat on, and off you go . . . oh, and may the best survivor win!

1. What do you call the pile of twigs and small sticks used to make a fire?

   a. Tinder

   b. Kindling

   c. Wigwam

2. The best way to light a fire outdoors is using a match and tinder. There are three other ways mentioned in this book. Two of these are listed here. Which is the odd one out?

a. Tapir

b. Magnifying glass

c. Flint

3. What's the best way to cook worms?

a. Boiling

b. Frying

c. Grilling

4. A good makeshift filter for purifying water is

a. A pair of underpants

b. A pair of socks

c. A T-shirt

5. If you haven't got a compass, what's the best item to help you find your way?

a. An atlas

b. A radio

c. A watch

6. The best way to help someone in difficulty in the water is

a. To reach them with a stick and pull them to safety

b. To swim to them and use a life-saving stroke to get them out

c. To shout the principles of good breast-stroke to them from the bank

7. A small child can drown in just
a. 3 inches (3.5 cm) of water
b. 6 inches (15 cm) of water
c. 9 inches (23 cm) of water

8. When escaping a fire, feel the back of a door before opening it. If it feels warm
a. Open it and fan it to and fro to cool it down
b. Open it a little to let some air in
c. Leave it shut

9. Normal body temperature is 98.6°F (37°C). In cases of hypothermia, death occurs when the body temperature drops to
a. 88°F (31°C)
b. 82° F (28°C)
c. 77°F (25°C)

10. Alligators and crocodiles can grow in length up to
a. Six feet (1.8 meters)
b. Twelve feet (3.6 meters)
c. Eighteen feet (5.5 meters)

11. If you find a casualty who is unconscious but breathing, you should put them
   a. In the recovery position
   b. In the foetal position
   c. In first position

12. The British SAS motto is
   a. Who Dares Wins
   b. Who Cares Who Wins?
   c. When the Going Gets Tough, the Tough Get Going

Piece of cake, huh? I knew you could do it. Let's see how many you got right then.

Answers

1b. **Kindling.** Tinder is the highly flammable material such as dry grass, dead leaves, or bark shavings that you put inside the kindling to light the fire. A wigwam is the style of fire because it resembles a wigwam cone shape when it's built.

2a. A tapir is a large animal found in South America and Southeast Asia, and has nothing to do with fires whatsoever. A taper, on the other hand, is quite handy for lighting fires but rarely in evidence in the wilds (more commonly found at Granny's fireside, in fact).

3a. **Boiling.** Frying is a luxury that you rarely have in the great outdoors unless you're well equipped with frying pan and oil. Worms tend to fall through the bars of a grill so stick to boiling.

4b. **Socks.** You could use underpants, I suppose, but rather you than me, old chap. A T-shirt has too many entrance and exit holes to be very practical but it could be used in an emergency.

5c. **Watch.** With an atlas, you'll be lucky to find the country you live in, let alone a detailed map of where you are now. A radio might keep your spirits up as you sing along to your favorite band, but unless it's a transmitter too (which is unlikely), it's not much good for finding your way home.

6a. **Reach first.** Remember, you swim to someone only as a last resort and if you're trained in life-saving techniques. The only way that shouting swimming lessons to people who are drowning could in any way be useful is to make them so mad that they somehow overcome their difficulties and get to the shore in order to thump you on the nose.

7a. Frighteningly enough, a child can drown in just 3 inches (7.5 cm) of water.

8c. Never open a door that feels warm to the touch: it means the fire is on the other side. A fire needs oxygen to burn. By keeping doors shut and sealed, you are preventing the fire from spreading.

9b. **82°F (28°C).** A casualty falls unconscious at 88°F (31°C) and would be well and truly deceased at 77°F (25°C).

10c. **Eighteen feet (5.5 meters).** Can you imagine having one of these monsters after you? You'd have to run the length of a bus just to get away from its teeth and down to its tail.

11a. **The recovery position** is the safest position for a casualty. The curled up foetal position may be comforting but not of much use medically. As for first position, this is neither the time nor the place for ballet. Better forget that one.

12a. **"Who Dares Wins"** is the **SAS** motto. And I wouldn't joke about it if I were you!

Full marks or not quite? I have no doubt that you got a respectable score and that you are now ready to meet the challenges that nature throws at you.

However, it is worth bearing in mind that most of the survivors we have heard about in this book did not go looking for trouble. They were simply unfortunate in finding themselves in grave danger and they used every resource at their fingertips to survive. You would have to be pretty foolish to deliberately put yourself in danger because wild nature can be a hostile place and you have to have skill, judgement, and luck on your side to negotiate the hazards.

I hope you've enjoyed the book and will remember some of the skills that we've discussed. Although you probably will never need any survival skills, I am safe in the knowledge that should a perilous situation arise, you'll be better prepared to cope with it than you were at the start of our adventure together.

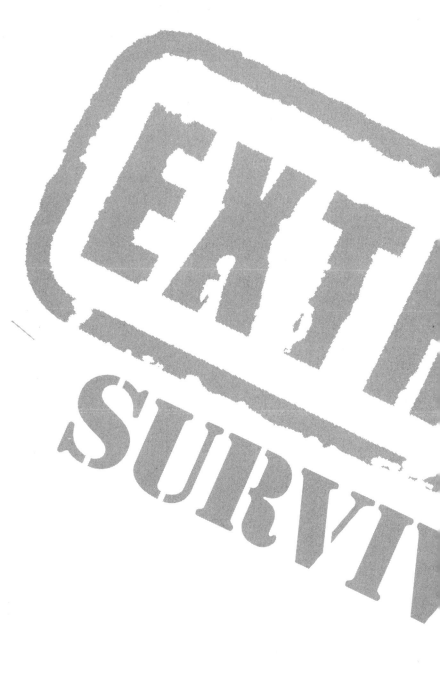